DEFINED

WHO GOD SAYS YOU ARE

A STUDY ON IDENTITY FOR KIDS

D1597386

OLDER KIDS ACTIVITY BOOK
STEPHEN & ALEX KENDRICK
LIFEWAY PRESS®
BRENTWOOD, TN

EDITORIAL TEAM
KIDS MINISTRY PUBLISHING

Chuck Peters
Director, Kids Ministry

Jeremy Carroll
Publishing Manager,
VBS and Kids Discipleship

Kayla Stevens
Publishing Team Leader
and Content Editor

Kathy Strawn
Writer

Sara Lansford
Production Editor

Stephanie Salvatore
Graphic Designer

Reprinted November 2022

ISBN: 978-1-535956-78-9
Item 005814775

Dewey Decimal Classification Number: 268.432
Subject Heading: Discipleship—Curricula\ God\Bible—Study
Dewey Decimal Classification Number: 248.82
Subject Heading: CHRISTIAN LIFE \ JESUS CHRIST—TEACHINGS

Printed in the United States of America
Lifeway Kids
Lifeway Resources
200 Powell Place, Suite 100
Brentwood, TN 37027-7707

We believe the Bible has God for its author; salvation for its end; and truth, without any mixture of error, for its matter and that all Scripture is totally true and trustworthy. To review Lifeway's doctrinal guideline, please visit lifeway.com/doctrinalguideline.

TABLE OF CONTENTS

AND YOU WERE DEAD IN YOUR TRESPASSES AND SINS IN WHICH YOU PREVIOUSLY LIVED ACCORDING TO THE WAYS OF THIS WORLD, ACCORDING TO THE RULER OF THE POWER OF THE AIR, THE SPIRIT NOW WORKING IN THE DISOBEDIENT. WE TOO ALL PREVIOUSLY LIVED AMONG THEM IN OUR FLESHLY DESIRES, CARRYING OUT THE INCLINATIONS OF OUR FLESH AND THOUGHTS, AND WE WERE BY NATURE CHILDREN UNDER WRATH AS THE OTHERS WERE ALSO.

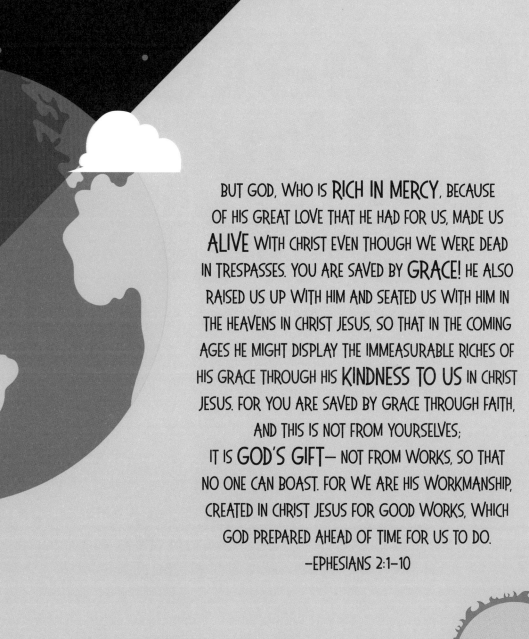

BUT GOD, WHO IS RICH IN MERCY, BECAUSE
OF HIS GREAT LOVE THAT HE HAD FOR US, MADE US
ALIVE WITH CHRIST EVEN THOUGH WE WERE DEAD
IN TRESPASSES. YOU ARE SAVED BY GRACE! HE ALSO
RAISED US UP WITH HIM AND SEATED US WITH HIM IN
THE HEAVENS IN CHRIST JESUS, SO THAT IN THE COMING
AGES HE MIGHT DISPLAY THE IMMEASURABLE RICHES OF
HIS GRACE THROUGH HIS KINDNESS TO US IN CHRIST
JESUS. FOR YOU ARE SAVED BY GRACE THROUGH FAITH,
AND THIS IS NOT FROM YOURSELVES;
IT IS GOD'S GIFT— NOT FROM WORKS, SO THAT
NO ONE CAN BOAST. FOR WE ARE HIS WORKMANSHIP,
CREATED IN CHRIST JESUS FOR GOOD WORKS, WHICH
GOD PREPARED AHEAD OF TIME FOR US TO DO.
–EPHESIANS 2:1–10

Created by God

CREATE—

to make, form, and bring into being

Only God is the true Creator.
He can create something
from nothing!

KNOW

God created people
in His image and for
His glory.

UNDERSTAND

God has the
authority to
determine our
identity and
purpose.

DISCOVER

The Bible helps us
know what being
created in God's
image means.

KEY VERSE: "FOR WE ARE HIS WORKMANSHIP,
CREATED IN CHRIST JESUS FOR GOOD WORKS,
WHICH GOD PREPARED AHEAD OF TIME FOR US TO DO."
—EPHESIANS 2:10

GOD CREATED PEOPLE

On the sixth day of creation, God created people. He said, "Let's make man in our image. They will rule over the whole earth and take care of all living creatures."

So God made man and woman in His image. God formed the man, Adam, from the dust of the ground. God breathed into him the breath of life. Adam became a living being. God placed Adam in the Garden of Eden where all kinds of trees grew. A river watered the garden. Adam worked the garden and took care of it. God told Adam, "You may eat from any tree in the garden except the tree of the knowledge of good and evil. If you eat from it, you will die."

Then God said, "It is not good for the man to be alone." So God decided to make a helper for the man. God brought all the animals to Adam, and Adam named them. But none of the animals was a good helper for the man. So God put Adam into a deep sleep. He took one of the man's ribs and closed the man's side. God took the rib and made a woman!

God took the woman to Adam. Adam was extremely happy when he saw Eve. "This one, at last," he said, "is bone of my bone and flesh of my flesh."

The woman was a perfect helper for the man; she was his wife.

God blessed Adam and Eve and provided everything they needed.

That was the end of the sixth day. On the seventh day, God stopped and rested because He had completed His work.

–based on Genesis 2

GOD MADE ME

Read each question, then write your answer on the question mark. Think about who God made you to be.

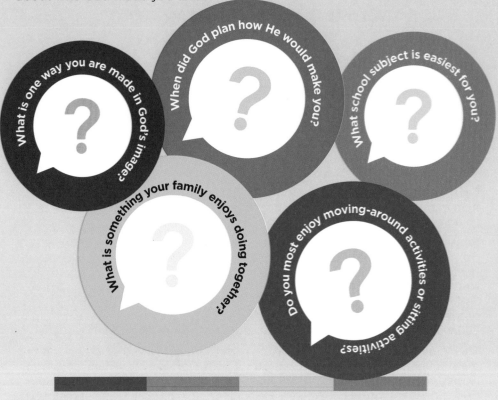

What is one way you are made in God's image?

When did God plan how He would make you?

What school subject is easiest for you?

What is something your family enjoys doing together?

Do you most enjoy moving-around activities or sitting activities?

🔍 DIGGING DEEPER

Knowing what God is like helps us know who He is. That is the beginning of knowing more about who God created us to be. Locate and read these verses, then make your own list telling what God is like. Then put a star next to your favorite one.

Psalm 46:1

Psalm 86:5

Psalm 86:10

1 John 4:8

Why did you choose the one with the star?

Think about your list as you answer this question: How am I made in God's image?

KEYBOARD CRAZINESS!

Can you crack the code to read the message on the tablet?

This means God is in total control!

YOUR TURN

Use the code (or create your own) to send a message about a way you are created in God's image.

MY DAILY JOURNAL

A journal is a place to keep track of your thoughts, feelings, questions, answers, and prayers. During the study, these pages will guide you to use your Bible, to think about what you read, and to give you suggestions for prayer.

READ GENESIS 1:1-27

As you read, write down everything God made that was mentioned.

Day 1: (vv. 1-5) ....

Day 2: (vv. 6-8) ....

Day 3: (vv. 9-13) ....

Day 4: (vv. 14-19) ....

Day 5: (vv. 20-23) ....

Day 6: (vv. 24-27) ....

What words come to mind about what God is like when you think about His creation? ....

....

Talk to God, naming several things you are thankful He made.

READ GENESIS 1:26-28

In whose image did God make people according to verse 27? ....

God is loving, creative, and kind. He made people with the ability to love, to create, and to be kind. Can you think of other ways God made people in His image? ....

....

....

....

God did not make people to be just like Him, but He did make them to have some qualities like Him. How do you feel about being made in God's image? Talk with God about your feelings. Ask Him questions you may have.

DAY 3

READ ACTS 17:24-27

Paul spoke these words to the Greeks in Athens. What did Paul know about God? List at least three things from these verses.

1) ....

2) ....

3) ....

How do you feel about the time and place in which God has placed you? Why might God have put you in the place you are right now? Where might God plan for you to live when you grow up? ....

....

....

....

DAY 4

READ PSALM 139:1-6

How well does God know you? Who might know you better than God? (If you need a hint, unscramble these words: *on eno*) ....

....

How do you feel knowing God knows everything about you? Are there things you wish He didn't know? Are there things you are glad He knows? ....

....

....

....

....

Even though God knows all about you, He likes to hear from you. Today, talk to God about your day, what went well and what didn't. Tell Him anything you want. He is ready to hear you.

READ JEREMIAH 1:4-8

God has loved you for a very long time. He has always had a plan for you. You may not know all of God's plan for you right now, but you do know some things He wants you to do.

Find and read these verses. Write what they tell you to do.

Psalm 107:1: ....

....

....

Luke 6:31: ....

....

....

Ephesians 4:32: ....

....

....

Ask God's help for what you need to do based on these verses. Remember that He has all power to help you. ....

....

....

....

....

....

CREATED BY GOD

What is God teaching you about Himself this week? What have you learned about yourself? Is there anything you need to spend time praying to God about?

Use this journal page to write out your prayers and any thoughts you have about what God is teaching you this week. Thank Him for teaching you through His Word.

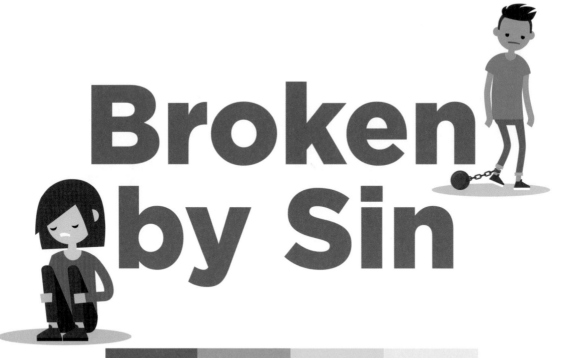

Broken by Sin

BROKEN—

Something that has been torn or fragmented

When people sin, they tear or break the relationship they had with God. They are separated from God by their sin. The good news is that God's plan provides the answer to the brokenness caused by sin.

KNOW

Sin is to think, say, or behave in any way that goes against God and His commands.

UNDERSTAND

All people are broken by sin.

DISCOVER

Before trusting Jesus, our identity is broken by our sin and rebellion against God.

KEY VERSE: "AND YOU WERE DEAD IN YOUR
TRESPASSES AND SINS."
—EPHESIANS 2:1

BROKEN BY SIN

ADAM AND EVE SINNED

One day a serpent approached Eve and asked, "Did God really say, 'You can't eat from any tree in the garden?'"

Eve corrected the serpent: "We may eat fruit from any tree except one in the middle of the garden. God said, 'You must not touch or eat that fruit, or you will die.'"

The serpent told Eve, "You won't die! In fact, God knows that when you eat it, you will be like Him, knowing good and evil."

Eve looked at the fruit on the tree. She remembered that the serpent said the fruit would make her wise. Eve took some of the fruit and ate it. She gave some to Adam, and he ate it, too.

Immediately, Adam and Eve realized what they had done. They tried to cover themselves and hide from God.

That evening, God called out to Adam. "Where are you? Did you eat from the tree I commanded you not to?"

Eve said, "The serpent tricked me, and I ate it."

God told the serpent, "Because you have done this, you are cursed more than any other animal. You will move on your belly and eat dust." Then God told Eve, "You will have pain when you have a baby." God told Adam, "You must work hard to grow your food now, and one day you will die."

God made Adam and Eve leave the garden.

—based on Genesis 3

IT'S A MATCH!

Gather different colored pencils, crayons, or markers. Shade in the boxes to the right using different colors. Put the pencils, crayons, or markers in a bag. Choose a Bible reference on the grid and pull out a pencil from the bag. If the color of the pencil matches the color of the box on the grid, you earn 5 points. If you find the verse and read it aloud, you earn the extra points shown on the box. If you can say the Bible verse from memory, you get double the points on the box!

HOW MANY POINTS DID YOU EARN? ☐

EPHESIANS 2:9	EPHESIANS 2:1–2	EPHESIANS 2:10
5 POINTS	**5 POINTS**	**10 POINTS**
EPHESIANS 2:4	EPHESIANS 2:8	EPHESIANS 2:3
15 POINTS	**20 POINTS**	**15 POINTS**
EPHESIANS 2:7	EPHESIANS 2:5	EPHESIANS 2:6
5 POINTS	**10 POINTS**	**15 POINTS**

LETTER LADDER

Answer the questions to discover a long word from Ephesians 2:1.

☐ WHAT LETTER IS SOMETHING TO DRINK?

☐ WHAT LETTER SOUNDS LIKE AN ANGRY PIRATE?

☐ WHAT LETTER COMES AFTER D?

☐ WHAT DO YOU ADD TO A WORD TO MAKE IT MEAN MORE THAN ONE?

☐ WHAT LETTER SOUNDS LIKE A VEGETABLE?

☐ WHAT IS THE VERY FIRST LETTER?

☐ WHAT IS THE 19TH LETTER?

☐ WHAT LETTER COMES BEFORE T?

☐ WHAT LETTER IS IN BOTH RED AND BLUE?

☐ WHAT LETTER IS DOUBLED TWICE IN MISSISSIPPI?

Some Bibles may use the word *transgressions*, but that word and the word you discovered in the puzzle mean the same as this 3-letter word: ☐ ☐ ☐

Find either word in these Bible verses as you read them.

Ephesians 2:1   Romans 5:18   Romans 3:23

CAN YOU READ IT?

Try reading these temptations and understanding them. If you need help, read the hint.

CAN YOU READ IT?

HINT:
WRITE THE
OPPOSITE
WORD ABOVE
WHAT'S
HIGHLIGHTED

BROKEN BY SIN

- Goodbye. Do I see money off the desk? Someone won't see me leave it.

- What are me down to? Me remembered my homework? I can't copy yours.

- Me can have a bad time. Me can't tease your sister. She is going in of school. Tell she that he's smart.

Now, decide how to handle each temptation so you won't be sinning!

[Answers: Hello. Do you see money on the desk? No one will see you take it. What are you up to? You forgot your homework? You can copy mine. We can have a good time. We can tease my brother. He is coming out of school. Tell him that he is dumb.]

DIGGING DEEPER

People often think the Bible is about people who always obeyed God. However, the Bible also tells us about times people did not obey Him. People are separated from God because of their sin. The good news is that... Wait! That comes next week!

Find each of these Bible passages. Write the name of the person in the verse and how each one sinned.

Numbers 20:7-11

2 Samuel 11:14-17; 12:10

Luke 19:8

Matthew 26:69-75

Acts 22:2-4

Now, think about this: Each one of those people was used by God in many wonderful ways later in their lives—even though they had sinned! When God forgives sin, He doesn't remember it anymore. (Hebrews 8:12)

MY DAILY JOURNAL

A journal is a place to keep track of your thoughts, feelings, questions, answers, and prayers. During the study, these pages will guide you to use your Bible, to think about what you read, and to give you suggestions for prayer.

READ EPHESIANS 2:1 AND GENESIS 3:1-2

As you read, note who was talking in the Genesis passage. Beside each name, write what that person said about God's command.

....

....

Why do you think the serpent wanted Eve to think about the fruit of the tree? ....

....

....

What happens when a person starts thinking about something that goes against God and His commands? ....

....

....

What kinds of things are you tempted to do that you should not? (Remember, you can write in code if you want your thoughts to be private.)

....

....

....

....

Talk to God, naming things that tempt you or might tempt you. Ask His help in overcoming temptation.

DAY 2

READ EPHESIANS 2:2 AND GENESIS 3:4-6

In each passage, Satan is described differently. What descriptions do you find?

1) ....

2) ....

Satan wants everyone to be separated from God all the time. He keeps working to trick people into sinning and disobeying God. Satan promised Eve that she would not die if she ate the fruit God had forbidden. Why do you think Eve trusted Satan instead of God? ....

....

Ephesians 2:2 tells how powerful Satan is. Satan is powerful, but he is not as powerful as God. Satan uses trickery. God uses honesty. How do you feel about that? ....

....

Talk with God about your feelings. Ask Him questions you may have.

DAY 3

READ EPHESIANS 2:3 AND GENESIS 3:6-7

How did Eve respond to the temptation to eat from the tree of the knowledge of good and evil? What did she do next? ....

....

Paul wanted the church in Ephesus to know that he and his companions had also faced temptations. Paul knew that every person sins and is separated from God. How do you think being separated from God might feel? ....

....

Talk with God about your feelings. Listen when He speaks to your heart and mind about how to say no to temptation. ....

....

Have you ever felt the separation from God because of sin? If so, talk with God about it. He is willing to forgive you when you trust Him as Savior and ask for forgiveness.

READ EPHESIANS 2:10 AND GENESIS 3:8-9

What good news do you find in Ephesians 2:10? ....

....

Who created Adam and Eve? According to Ephesians 2:10, what did God create Adam and Eve to do? ....

....

How did Adam and Eve not follow God's plan? ....

....

According to Ephesians 2:10, what has God created you to do? ....

....

How do you feel knowing God created you for specific good works? ....

....

Talk to God about your feelings. Ask what He wants you to do.

READ EPHESIANS 2:12 AND GENESIS 3:10-13

Paul pointed out that when people were without Jesus, they had no hope for anything but separation brought on by sin. How do you feel when you are separated from someone you love? ....

....

....

Adam and Eve did not want to admit what they had done. Who blamed who? Fill in these blanks for what they did.

.... blamed .... blamed ....

.... caused all the blame.

What is God teaching you about Himself this week? What have you learned about yourself? Is there anything you need to spend time praying to God about?

Use this journal page to write out your prayers and any thoughts you have about what God is teaching you this week. Thank Him for teaching you through His Word.

Transformed by the Gospel

TRANSFORMED—
changed completely

When a person trusts Jesus as Savior, he is changed completely. He is forgiven of sins, adopted into God's family, wants to act differently, and is full of God's love.

KNOW

Trusting in Jesus for salvation transforms your identity.

UNDERSTAND

God's salvation is eternal. Nothing can separate believers from God's love.

DISCOVER

God's salvation is a gift that every person needs and can receive.

KEY VERSE: "FOR YOU ARE SAVED BY GRACE THROUGH FAITH,
AND THIS IS NOT FROM YOURSELVES; IT IS GOD'S GIFT—
NOT FROM WORKS, SO THAT NO ONE CAN BOAST."
—EPHESIANS 2:8–9

SAUL'S CONVERSION

Saul was an enemy of those who believed in Jesus. Saul entered house after house and dragged the believers away to prison. He made murderous threats against Jesus' followers, requesting permission from the high priest to travel to Damascus and arrest believers there.

As Saul was near Damascus, a bright light from heaven flashed around him. The light blinded Saul, and he fell to the ground. He heard a voice ask: "Why are you persecuting (hurting) Me?" "Who are You, Lord?" Saul asked.

"I am Jesus, the One you are persecuting," was the answer. "Go into the city. You will be told what to do."

Saul's traveling partners led him to the city. He could not see for three days. God told a man named Ananias, "Go to Saul. He has been praying. He knows you are coming to help him see again."

Ananias replied, "Lord, I have heard how much evil this man has done." God replied, "Go because I have chosen this man to tell the Gentiles about Me!" Ananias obeyed. When he put his hands on Saul's eyes, Saul could see again. Saul was baptized and immediately began to preach in the synagogues about Jesus. "Jesus is God's Son!" Saul announced.

Some Jews were angry with Saul's new message. They plotted to kill him. Saul's friends helped him escape Damascus by lowering him over the wall in a basket. Saul went back to Jerusalem and continued to speak boldly about his faith in Jesus.

—based on Acts 9:1-20

ODDS OR EVENS

Discover the answers to the words in the blanks. Begin at *Start*. Move only to even-numbered squares that touch. As you go, write the letter printed in each square along the path.

GOD'S ☐☐☐☐☐☐☐☐☐ IS

☐☐☐☐☐☐

21 E	19 X	331 B	104 N	98 R	38 E	6 T
		502 L	444 A			18 E
				28 O	54 N	55 U	22 P
110 I		56 V	44 A	36 I	
32 M		17 F	31 B	94 T	100 A	70 V
70 X	75 P	9 E	101 S			32 L
123 A	60 Z	81 G		19 X	54 A
5 R		29 N	40 E	6 C	2 S
1 A	64 E	421 I	11 H	93 T	67 O	5 N	START
98 R	97 E	503 T	18 S		

Now, begin at Start again. This time move only to odd-numbered squares that touch. As you go, write the letter printed in each square in order.

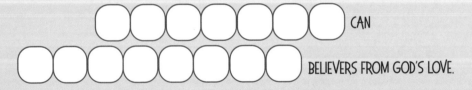

☐☐☐☐☐☐☐ CAN

☐☐☐☐☐☐☐ BELIEVERS FROM GOD'S LOVE.

COMPASS POINTS

Follow the compass directions to find the missing words from these statements about Saul. Follow the directions on each line to get to the next letter. (North is up; South is down; West is left, East is right.) Print it and start the next line of directions.

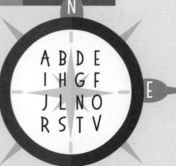

Compass grid:

```
A B D E
I H G F
J L N O
R S T V
```

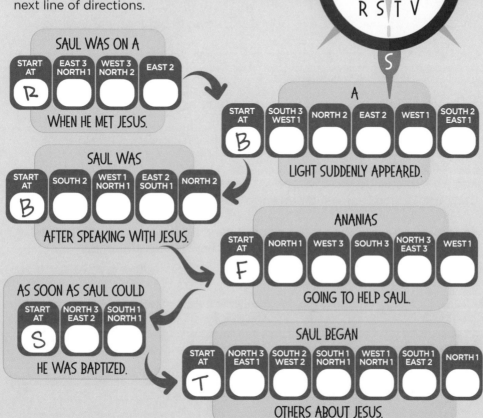

SAUL WAS ON A

START AT	EAST 3 NORTH 1	WEST 3 NORTH 2	EAST 2
R			

WHEN HE MET JESUS.

A

START AT	SOUTH 3 WEST 1	NORTH 2	EAST 2	WEST 1	SOUTH 2 EAST 1
B					

LIGHT SUDDENLY APPEARED.

SAUL WAS

START AT	SOUTH 2	WEST 1 NORTH 1	EAST 2 SOUTH 1	NORTH 2
B				

AFTER SPEAKING WITH JESUS.

ANANIAS

START AT	NORTH 1	WEST 3	SOUTH 3	NORTH 3 EAST 3	WEST 1
F					

GOING TO HELP SAUL.

AS SOON AS SAUL COULD

START AT	NORTH 3 EAST 2	SOUTH 1 NORTH 1
S		

HE WAS BAPTIZED.

SAUL BEGAN

START AT	NORTH 3 EAST 1	SOUTH 2 WEST 2	SOUTH 1 NORTH 1	WEST 1 NORTH 1	SOUTH 1 EAST 2	NORTH 1
T						

OTHERS ABOUT JESUS.

 DIGGING DEEPER

Read Acts 9:1 and then Acts 9:20. Notice what Saul was like before meeting Jesus, then what he was like after meeting Jesus.

BEFORE:	AFTER:

When Paul wrote to the Ephesians, he described what people are like before they trust Jesus and what they are like afterward. Read Ephesians 5:1-6. In the *Before* column, write the verse numbers that describe people before trusting Jesus. In the *After* column, write the verse numbers that describe people after trusting Jesus.

MY DAILY JOURNAL

A journal is a place to keep track of your thoughts, feelings, questions, answers, and prayers. During the study, these pages will guide you to use your Bible, to think about what you read, and to give you suggestions for prayer.

DAY 1

READ ACTS 9:1-3

Saul was a religious man. He tried to do everything God's law commanded. Saul did not believe Jesus was God's Son. What bad things was Saul doing?

....

....

Why do you think Jesus met Saul on the road to Damascus? ....

....

Even though Saul did not love Jesus, Jesus loved Saul. Salvation is a gift every person needs and can receive. Jesus wanted Saul's identity to be transformed from sinful and broken to child of God.

You have God's attention when you pray, and He has your attention. Talk to God about your own actions and whether they honor God or not. ....

....

....

DAY 2

READ ACTS 9:4-9

Jesus called Saul by name. What question did He ask of Saul? ....

....

What name did Saul call Jesus? ....

Saul knew he was talking to someone special. How did Jesus make sure Saul knew who He was? ....

....

Today, God usually speaks through prayer and the Bible. What are some things you have learned from the Bible that God wants you to do? ....

....

....

Ask God to help you always do what He wants you to do. Consider asking Him to teach you more about His plans for you. Talk with God about your feelings. Ask Him questions you may have.

READ ACTS 9:10-14

Ananias was one of Jesus' disciples who lived in Damascus. He didn't seem surprised when the Lord called his name, but he may have been surprised when he found out what the Lord wanted him to do. What was it?

Why was Ananias concerned about going to Saul?

Sometimes people are still afraid to do what God wants. They may fear telling others about Jesus, standing up for someone who needs help, or refusing to go along with friends who make wrong choices.

Do you sometimes fear what will happen if you do what God wants you to do? Explain.

God knows how you feel. Talk to Him about your concerns and fears.

Read Isaiah 41:10. Remember that even when you are afraid, God is always with you!

READ ACTS 9:15-20

Even though Ananias was worried about going to Saul, he obeyed God. What clue do you find in verse 17 that Ananias realized Saul has changed? (Need a hint? Look at what Ananias called him.)

Saul must have been hungry after three days without food, but he didn't eat first. Unscramble these letters to find out what he did do first.

SAUL WAS [＿＿＿＿＿] TIZBAPED

Saul was truly changed. What do you find in verse 20 that proves that?

Have you been completely changed by God? If so, thank God for that. If not, talk to God about any questions or uncertainties you have. He is ready to give you answers.

READ EPHESIANS 2:8-9

These verses have some words that are not always easy to understand:

GRACE is love and acceptance from God. It is free to us. We cannot ever work hard enough to get it.

FAITH is belief or trust in something or someone. In these verses, faith is belief or trust in Jesus.

WORKS means deeds or actions. The Bible tells us that no one can do enough good works to earn God's forgiveness. Only trust in Jesus as Savior will save a person from the punishment of sin.

Memorize Ephesians 2:8-9 and recite these verses to a friend or family member this week.

What is God teaching you about Himself this week? What have you learned about yourself? Is there anything you need to spend time praying to God about?

Use this journal page to write out your prayers and any thoughts you have about what God is teaching you this week. Thank Him for teaching you through His Word.

Who We Are in Christ

NEW IDENTITY
BELIEVER

ADOPTED—
taken or chosen as one's own

When a person trusts in Jesus as Savior, God brings that person into His family as His own son or daughter.

KNOW
You are who God says you are.

UNDERSTAND
Everyone who trusts in Jesus receives a new identity.

DISCOVER
God defines the true identity of all followers of Jesus.

KEY VERSE: "BUT GOD, WHO IS RICH IN MERCY,
BECAUSE OF HIS GREAT LOVE THAT HE HAD FOR US, MADE US ALIVE WITH CHRIST
EVEN THOUGH WE WERE DEAD IN TRESPASSES. YOU ARE SAVED BY GRACE!"
—EPHESIANS 2:4–5

THE VINE AND THE BRANCHES

Jesus said, "I am the true vine. My Father is the gardener. The gardener cuts off every branch in Me that does not produce fruit. However, if a branch is producing fruit, He prunes it (cuts off just the dead parts) so the branch can continue to produce fruit."

Then Jesus reminded His disciples they are already followers of Him. Jesus told His disciples He wanted them to remain in Him, just like a healthy branch produces fruit when it stays attached to the vine. He explained that He would remain in them, too. He pointed out that a branch broken off the vine cannot produce any fruit but must stay connected to the vine in order to produce fruit.

Again, Jesus repeated, "I am the vine." This time, however, He added that His followers were the branches. He urged them to remain in Him in order to produce much fruit. He said, "Without Me, you can do nothing. If you don't remain in Me, you are like one of the branches that is carried off to be burned up."

Jesus encouraged the believers to remain in Him and in His words. "God is glorified when you produce much fruit and show that you are My disciples," Jesus said.

—based on John 15:1-8

WHO WE ARE IN CHRIST

TRUE IDENTITY

Each identity card describes something about all believers. Write the letter that comes before each letter in the alphabet to find some of those descriptions.

A B C D E F G H I J K L M N O P Q R S T U V W X Y Z

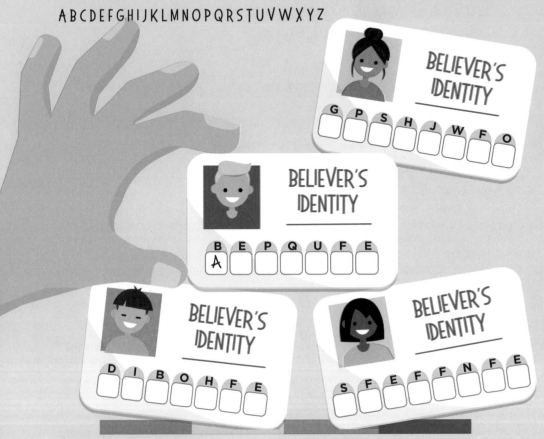

BELIEVER'S IDENTITY
G P S H J W F O

BELIEVER'S IDENTITY
B E P Q U F E
A

BELIEVER'S IDENTITY
D I B O H F E

BELIEVER'S IDENTITY
S F E F F N F E

DIGGING DEEPER

Read Ephesians 2:4-5. List what is true about God and list what is true about you.

GOD:

YOU:

According to these verses, how is a person saved when he trusts Jesus as Savior and Lord? Unscramble these five words to find out if you are right.

OUY   ERA   VASDE   YB   RCGAE

FOLLOW THE VINES

Each vine has a trail of letters. You need some of the letters to form answers to the questions. Choose a vine. Look at the first letter on the vine. Cross it out each time it is on the vine. The other letters spell a word from today's Bible story. Write the answer in the space below the question.

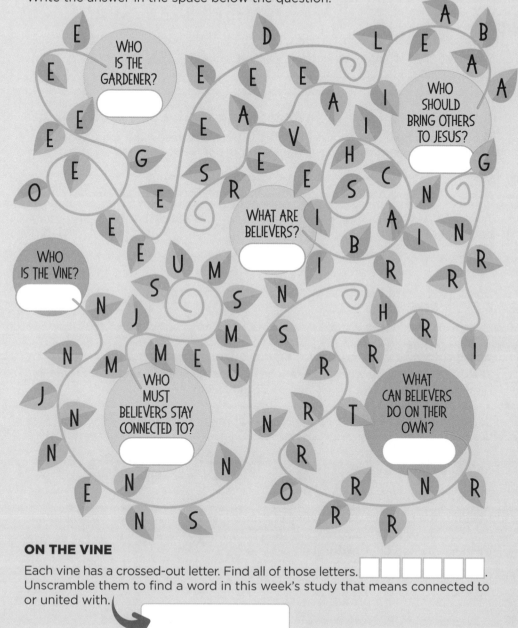

WHO IS THE GARDENER?

WHO SHOULD BRING OTHERS TO JESUS?

WHAT ARE BELIEVERS?

WHO IS THE VINE?

WHO MUST BELIEVERS STAY CONNECTED TO?

WHAT CAN BELIEVERS DO ON THEIR OWN?

ON THE VINE

Each vine has a crossed-out letter. Find all of those letters. ☐☐☐☐☐☐☐.
Unscramble them to find a word in this week's study that means connected to or united with.

MY DAILY JOURNAL

A journal is a place to keep track of your thoughts, feelings, questions, answers, and prayers. During the study, these pages will guide you to use your Bible, to think about what you read, and to give you suggestions for prayer.

DAY 1

READ JOHN 15:1

What are some things you know a gardener does? ....

....

Jesus used a parable or story when He described His Father as the gardener. Think about how close the relationship is between Jesus and God. What words come to mind when you think about that relationship? ....

....

Talk to God with a praise prayer, naming good things about Him. Make notes here if you want. ....

....

....

DAY 2

READ JOHN 15:2-4

Jesus told about the vine and branches to encourage believers to remain in Him—to continue growing to look more like Jesus.

Look at these phrases. Circle the ones that mean the same as REMAIN IN.

CONNECTED TO   APART FROM   STAY WITH   UNITED WITH

Reading the Bible, praying, thinking about Jesus and God, and choosing to obey are ways to remain in Jesus. Talk with God, asking Him to help you stay connected and united with Him. ....

....

....

READ JOHN 15:5-6

Who is Jesus speaking to in these verses? To find out, use an alphabet code where each number stands for a letter, in order, of the alphabet.

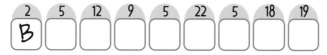

2 — B
5
12
9
5
22
5
18
19

The fruit Jesus taught about was not apples and oranges. The fruit of believers is bringing people to learn about and trust Jesus. Good fruit also means growing in Jesus and trusting Him more.

Pray, thanking Jesus that He helps you do these things when you stay united with Him.

READ JOHN 15:7-8

You might think verse 7 means a believer can ask for anything and get it. Instead, when a person is truly connected to and united with Jesus, the things he wants to ask God for change. A believer wants to ask God for the things Jesus wants to happen. What kind of things might that be?

Remember that Jesus wants what is best for you. He has a good plan for your life to worship Him, love Him, and bring Him glory.

Today, talk to God about ways you can live in a way to love God and bring Him glory. Thank God that you can always talk to Him about anything.

WHO WE ARE IN CHRIST

READ EPHESIANS 2:4-5

Think about the meaning of these words you read. Decide what each one means. Draw a line from each word to its meaning. (The answers are at the bottom of the page.)

GRACE   NOT RECEIVING PUNISHMENT YOU DESERVE

FAITH   RECEIVING WHAT YOU DO NOT DESERVE

MERCY   TRUST OR BELIEF

What wonderful gifts God gives to us! Thank Him for each of these blessings.

....

....

....

Grace (2), Faith (3), Mercy (1)

What is God teaching you about Himself this week? What have you learned about yourself? Is there anything you need to spend time praying to God about?

Use this journal page to write out your prayers and any thoughts you have about what God is teaching you this week. Thank Him for teaching you through His Word.

What We Have in Christ

LOST—
describes people without God

Although all people sin, not all people trust Jesus to save them from the punishment of their sin. Those who have not believed that Jesus is the only way to be a child of God are described as lost. People who have trusted Jesus are described as saved.

KNOW

When we trust in Jesus, God adopts us and welcomes us into His family as His children.

UNDERSTAND

Jesus came to seek and to save the lost.

DISCOVER

We receive the blessing of eternal life as an inheritance from God.

JESUS TAUGHT THREE PARABLES

Tax collectors and sinners came to listen to Jesus teach. The religious leaders complained because Jesus welcomed sinners, so Jesus told them three parables to teach them about God.

Jesus said, "If a man has 100 sheep and loses one, what does he do? He leaves the 99 sheep in the open field and searches for the lost sheep until he finds it. Then he tells his friends, 'Let's celebrate! I found my lost sheep!'" Then Jesus said, "This is what heaven is like; there is more joy in heaven when one sinner repents and turns back to God than for 99 people who did not wander off."

Jesus said, "If a woman has 10 silver coins and loses one of them, what does she do? She lights a lamp, sweeps the house, and searches carefully until she finds it! Then she tells her friends, 'Let's celebrate! I found my lost coin!'" Then Jesus said, "This is what heaven is like. There is joy in heaven when one sinner repents and turns back to God."

Finally, Jesus said, "A man had two sons. The younger son said, 'Father, give me my inheritance today.' So the father gave his son his share. The younger son left home. He wasted his money and lived foolishly. There was a famine, and the people there did not have enough food. The son got a job feeding pigs. He was so hungry, even the pigs' food looked tasty."

"The younger son made a plan. He would go back to his father and admit he was wrong. He would ask to work for his father like the servants."

"So the younger son headed home. He was still a long way away when his father saw him coming. His father ran to him, threw his arms around him, and kissed him. The son began to apologize. 'I have sinned against God and against you,' he said."

"But the father told his servants, 'Let's celebrate with a feast! Bring the best robe and put it on my son! Put a ring on his finger and sandals on his feet. This son of mine was lost, and now he is found!'"

"At this time, the older son came from the fields and heard music at the house. 'What's going on?' he asked one of the servants."

"'Your brother is here,' the servant said. 'Your father is celebrating.' "The older brother was angry! He refused to go to the feast. The father asked him to come inside. 'Look!' the older brother said. 'I never disobeyed you! But you never threw a party for me.'"

"'Son,' the father said, 'everything I have is yours. We have to celebrate and be happy. Your brother was lost and is found.'"

—based on Luke 15

DIGGING DEEPER:

The Book of Ephesians is a letter Paul wrote to the Christians in the city of Ephesus. Paul was probably in prison in Rome while he wrote this letter. Ephesians tells readers about Christ, His church, the Holy Spirit, salvation, and how to live the Christian life. Find each of these verses and write beside the reference which of those things is mentioned.

Ephesians 1:9

Ephesians 1:13

Ephesians 3:10

Ephesians 2:8

Ephesians 4:25-26

In what way can the messages in Ephesians help you?

COLOR CUES

Use one color to fill in the words that appear in Ephesians 2:6.
Use another color to fill in words that appear in Ephesians 2:7.
Use a third color to fill in words that appear in both verses.

Use the words to help you recall and say the verses by memory. Are there words you don't understand? If so, ask your teacher or a parent to help you know what the verses mean.

LOST AND FOUND WORD SEARCH

Find in the puzzle the words from the Word Box. Some of the words are from the Bible story and some are words that tell what a person has when he trusts Jesus as Savior.

WORD BOX
ADOPTION
COIN
FATHER
FORGIVENESS
HOLY SPIRIT
HUNT
LOST
REDEMPTION
SHEEP
SON

```
F F B Q T F S P H D T
V R A E S A F E V A G I
T J Z O T X I N I A G R
T Y L H G R J R I D H I
S S E N E V I G R O F P
W R Z A R S T V I P C S
X P E E H S N W B T O Y
P W I J K Y U T I I G L
T P J S T K H R V O H O
R E D E M P T I O N H H
S O N S Y Q O I Z H O K
U X R O C W R H C P J Z
```

LOST THINGS

Close your eyes and try to touch the gameboard with your finger. Open your eyes and see where your finger landed. Tell about someone who was in the Bible story, something that happened in the Bible story, or why something in the story happened. If you are playing alone, take another turn. If you are playing with someone else, let the other person take a turn. Try to answer a different question each time.

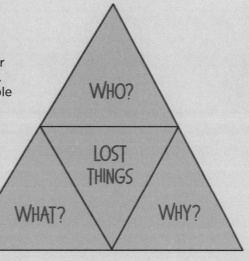

WHO?

LOST THINGS

WHAT?   WHY?

MY DAILY JOURNAL

A journal is a place to keep track of your thoughts, feelings, questions, answers, and prayers. During the study, these pages will guide you to use your Bible, to think about what you read, and to give you suggestions for prayer.

READ LUKE 15:3-7

Draw what the man lost and then found. Draw on the man's face the way you think he felt when he found what was lost.

Jesus told a story about sheep, but He wanted the people to learn something about Him. He wanted people to know that He was looking for those who are lost (without God) and wanted to save them (bring them to God).

Thank God for sending Jesus to look for those who need Him and to provide salvation for those who ask Him.

READ LUKE 15:8-10

Draw what was lost and then found in this story. How did the woman feel when she found what was lost?

The second story Jesus told is about money, but He wanted the people to learn something about Him. What do you think He wanted them to learn? ....

....

Match these words with their definitions. Use the words in your answer to the question above.

LOST   RESCUED FROM THE PUNISHMENT OF SIN
SAVED   PEOPLE WITHOUT GOD

Praise Jesus for coming to earth to die, be buried, be resurrected, and return to heaven. Write your thoughts about the story of the lost coin and about the joy Jesus has when someone trusts Him for salvation. ....

....

....

READ LUKE 15:11-24

In this Bible story told by Jesus, the father did not misplace his son, but he did not know where his son was. How did the father react when his son came home? Circle things the father gave his son. ....

....

ROBE   CAMELS   RING   SANDALS   WATER JUGS   FOOD

How do you think the father felt when his son came back? ....

....

When Jesus comes to anyone who is lost (without God) and brings them to God, He feels great joy just like the people in the three stories in Luke 15.

Do you know anyone who is without God? If so, pray that the person will come to know God. Ask God how you can help the person come to God. If you thought of someone who is lost, print his initials in this box. Begin to pray for this person every day.

READ LUKE 15:25-31

The father was glad to see his younger son, but how did the older brother feel?

....

....

What two things did the brother complain about in verses 29-30?

1) ....

2) ....

Which brother do you think pleased his father the most?

☐ YOUNGER ☐ OLDER

When you pray today, talk to God about ways to be sure you aren't jealous or angry about the good others are getting. Ask Him to help you be glad for what others have and thankful for what you have.

READ EPHESIANS 1:3-13

Sometimes when people trust Jesus as Savior, they think most about God's promise of eternal life with Him, but there are many more blessings! What two blessings do you find in verse 7?

1) ....

2) ....

How many blessings can you count in today's Bible passage? ....

....

If you have already trusted Jesus as Savior and Lord, thank Him for the blessings you have. If you have not yet trusted Jesus as Savior and Lord, tell Him why you are waiting. ....

....

....

....

....

DEFINED

What is God teaching you about Himself this week? What have you learned about yourself? Is there anything you need to spend time praying to God about?

Use this journal page to write out your prayers and any thoughts you have about what God is teaching you this week. Thank Him for teaching you through His Word.

Living Out Our Identity

IDENTITY IN CHRIST —
Who God says you are

When a person becomes a Christian, her identity is changed. The person looks the same on the outside, but she is a different person in the ways she thinks, feels, and acts.

KNOW

We are responsible for our choices.

UNDERSTAND

Christians still sin because we have hearts that want to sin, but we can say no to sin by asking God for help.

DISCOVER

As disciples we grow in our faith and knowledge of Jesus.

KEY VERSE: "IN WHICH YOU PREVIOUSLY LIVED ACCORDING TO THE WAYS OF THIS WORLD, ACCORDING TO THE RULER OF THE POWER OF THE AIR, THE SPIRIT NOW WORKING IN THE DISOBEDIENT. WE TOO ALL PREVIOUSLY LIVED AMONG THEM IN OUR FLESHLY DESIRES, CARRYING OUT THE INCLINATIONS OF OUR FLESH AND THOUGHTS, AND WE WERE BY NATURE CHILDREN UNDER WRATH AS THE OTHERS WERE ALSO." –EPHESIANS 2:2–3

PETER DENIED JESUS AND WAS FORGIVEN

On the night before Jesus was crucified, Peter shared the Passover supper with Jesus and the other disciples. Jesus said, "Peter, Satan will test you, but I have prayed that your faith will not fail." Jesus encouraged Peter to come back to the disciples afterward and to help them be faithful.

Peter said, "Lord, I am ready to go with you to prison or to die."

Jesus said, "Before the rooster crows today, you will deny three times that you even know Me."

Later that night, Jesus was arrested. Peter followed and waited outside. A servant girl said, "This man was with Jesus." Peter quickly said, "I don't know Him!" Someone else said, "You're one of His followers!" Peter said, "No, I am not!"

A third person said, "He is from Galilee. He was with Jesus." Peter said, "I don't know what you are talking about!" Just then, the rooster crowed. Jesus turned and looked at Peter. Peter ran away, crying over what he had done.

But the story isn't over! After Jesus' resurrection, Peter and other disciples were fishing. They had not caught any fish all night long. At sunrise, Jesus stood on the shore, but the disciples didn't recognize Him. Jesus told the men to throw their net on the other side of the boat to find fish. As soon as they did, the net was full of fish!

One of the disciples said, "It is the Lord!" Peter jumped into the water and hurried ashore before the others. The men ate breakfast on the shore with Jesus.

Three times, Jesus asked Peter, "Do you love me?" Three times, Peter answered, "Yes. You know I do!" Three times Jesus told Peter to feed His sheep, meaning for Peter to take care of Jesus' followers.

Three times Peter had denied knowing Jesus and now three times Jesus asked if Peter loved Him. Three times Jesus told Peter there was still work for him to do.

Later, Peter was with the other disciples in Jerusalem when the Holy Spirit came on them and they spoke in many languages. When people wondered what was happening, Peter preached to the crowd. He told them about Jesus. He begged the listeners to believe in Jesus as Savior. About 3000 people became believers that day!

Years later, when Paul wrote a letter to the Colossians, he urged believers to live lives that were true to what Jesus and the Scripture taught. Paul challenged the people to be compassionate, kind, humble, gentle, and patient. "Do everything in the name of Jesus," Paul wrote.

–based on Luke 22:31-34; 54-62; John 21:1-19; Acts 2, Colossians 3

LIVING OUT OUR IDENTITY

SORT IT OUT

Begin at box 1. Print on the blanks the letters from the box. Keep going with box 2 and so on. Then read the verse aloud. Practice reading it with a friend. Read it once with your teacher.

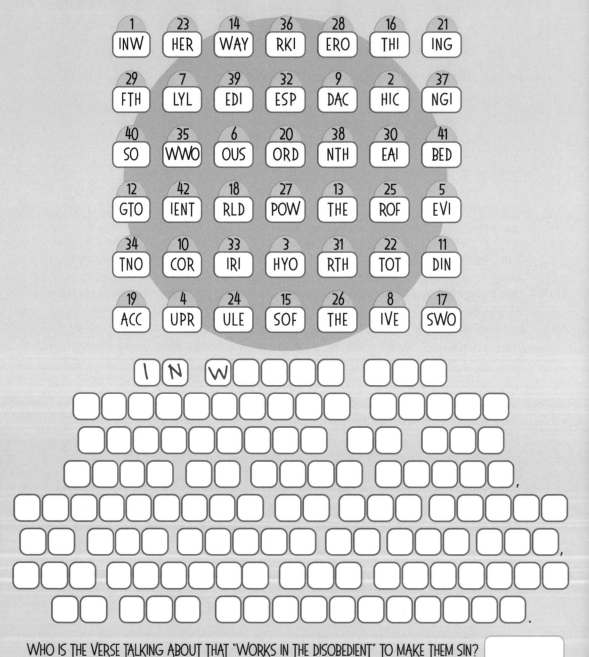

WHO IS THE VERSE TALKING ABOUT THAT "WORKS IN THE DISOBEDIENT" TO MAKE THEM SIN?

DIGGING DEEPER

Locate Ephesians 4:17-32 in your Bible. Read the verses. As you read, list the things a Christian should try to stop doing under the "Thumbs Down" column. List things a Christian should try to do under the "Thumbs Up" column. Which do you think is harder: to stop doing something wrong or to start doing something right?

THUMBS UP!   **THUMBS DOWN!**

ABOUT ME

Use a colored marker or pencil to shade in all of the shapes that contain a dot. Use the word you discover in the sentence. You will find out something about yourself!

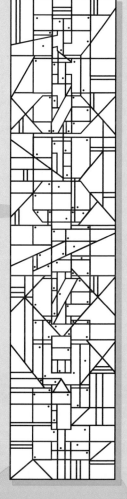

PETER AND JESUS

What question did Jesus ask Peter three times?

How many times did Peter answer Jesus?

How many times did Jesus tell Peter he had work to do for God?

How many times did Peter deny knowing Jesus?

What do the answers to these questions make you think?

Hint: The words surrounding the questions give you the answers!

I AM .... FOR MY CHOICES.

MY DAILY JOURNAL

A journal is a place to keep track of your thoughts, feelings, questions, answers, and prayers. During the study, these pages will guide you to use your Bible, to think about what you read, and to give you suggestions for prayer.

DAY 1

READ LUKE 22:31-34

Jesus used Peter's other name here. What name is it? ....

Jesus knew something about Peter that Peter didn't know. Look in verse 34 for what it is. ....

....

Peter thought he was ready to follow Jesus—even to die or go to prison. Peter really meant what he said. He intended to keep his promise, but Jesus knew what was going to happen.

Today, praise God for knowing what is happening and what will happen. Ask Him to help you do your best to always be ready to follow Jesus. ....

....

....

....

....

DAY 2

READ LUKE 22:54-62

Which of these emotions do you think Peter had during these events?

FEAR   ANGER   SADNESS   JOY   NERVOUSNESS

Which emotion do you think Jesus had? ....

....

Peter knew he had done wrong. He knew, and Jesus knew. He was truly sorry for what he had done. That is the first part of repentance. The second part is turning to Jesus for help.

When you pray today, think about your day. Did you do, say, or think anything that was not good? Think about the fact that Jesus knows what you did. If you mean it, tell God about your sorrow over what you did.

....

....

....

DAY 3

READ JOHN 21:15-17

Write Jesus' question to Peter here:

....

Write Peter's answer to Jesus here:

....

Write Jesus' directions to Peter here:

....

God can always use a person who loves, trusts, and follows Him. Even if that person has sinned, God can forgive him and give him joy in his life. However, if the person sinned but never talks to God about it or asks forgiveness, his life will never be as full.

....

....

Today, thank God for the fact that He restores people when they ask. Ask Him to help you remember to ask Him for forgiveness when it is needed.

....

....

....

DAY 4

READ ACTS 2:1-4

Peter and the disciples were in a room together when the Holy Spirit came on them. What could people see when this happened? ....

....

What two things could people hear? ....

Jesus had promised the Holy Spirit—and He came in a way no one could miss! People in the city wondered how they could hear the disciples preaching in all those languages. When confusion arose, Peter stood to speak. He was no longer afraid to say he knew Jesus. Look in Acts 2:22 to find what Peter had to say now. ....

....

Ask God to give you boldness to tell others about Him. Ask God to give you courage to openly obey Him no matter the circumstances. ....

....

DAY 5

READ EPHESIANS 4:32

This verse shows what you are supposed to do as a Christian. What are some ways you can be kind and caring to your friends? ....

....

What are some ways you can be kind and caring to people who are not your friends? ....

....

How can you care for someone who lives with you? ....

....

What does Paul mention in the verse as the reason that you should be kind, caring, and forgiving? ....

....

Pray today thanking God for His forgiveness and asking Him to help you forgive others. ....

....

What is God teaching you about Himself this week? What have you learned about yourself? Is there anything you need to spend time praying to God about?

Use this journal page to write out your prayers and any thoughts you have about what God is teaching you this week. Thank Him for teaching you through His Word.

Walking in the Spirit

FRUIT OF THE SPIRIT-
the results of the Holy Spirit's workings in the lives of believers

When a person is guided by the Holy Spirit, the results are peace, love, joy, patience, kindness, goodness, faithfulness, gentleness, and self-control.

KNOW

The Holy Spirit guides us as we live for God's glory.

UNDERSTAND

The Holy Spirit shows us our sin and helps us make God-honoring choices.

DISCOVER

The Holy Spirit changes the way we think and act to be more like Jesus.

KEY VERSE: "IN WHICH YOU PREVIOUSLY LIVED ACCORDING TO THE WAYS OF THIS WORLD, ACCORDING TO THE RULER OF THE POWER OF THE AIR, THE SPIRIT NOW WORKING IN THE DISOBEDIENT. WE TOO ALL PREVIOUSLY LIVED AMONG THEM IN OUR FLESHLY DESIRES, CARRYING OUT THE INCLINATIONS OF OUR FLESH AND THOUGHTS, AND WE WERE BY NATURE CHILDREN UNDER WRATH AS THE OTHERS WERE ALSO." –EPHESIANS 2:2–3

THE FRUIT OF THE SPIRIT

Paul wrote a letter to the Christians in Galatia. Galatia was a province in Rome, and many of the Christians there were Gentiles, or non-Jews. Paul explained that God changes people who trust in Jesus. God gives them the Holy Spirit, who guides them and gives them power to become more like Jesus. Paul wrote that the Holy Spirit changes the way we think and act. He wanted believers to know that if you let the Holy Spirit guide you, you will do what God wants instead of what you want.

When sin is in control, we do wrong things. We show hatred, jealousy, anger, selfishness, and greed. We fight and get into trouble. People who live like this will not enter God's kingdom. But Jesus frees us from the power of sin. His Holy Spirit lives in us and gives us power to do what is right.

When the Holy Spirit is in control, people choose love, joy, peace, patience, kindness, goodness, faithfulness, gentleness, and self-control. These actions are the fruit of the Spirit—proof that the Spirit is in someone—like how a healthy tree produces fruit. This fruit pleases God. Paul wrote that when we trust in Jesus, we no longer want to do whatever pleases ourselves. The Holy Spirit gives us power to say no to things like hatred, jealousy, anger, selfishness, and greed. The more we know Jesus, the more we will choose actions like joy, kindness, and self-control. We will want to live to please God. Since the Holy Spirit lives in us, we must let the Holy Spirit guide us.

—based on Galatians 5

WALKING IN THE SPIRIT

TEXT MESSAGE FOR YOU

In Ephesians 2:2-3, Paul tells what people are like before trusting Jesus. Fill in the missing words from these verses on the phone screens. Number them in the correct order.

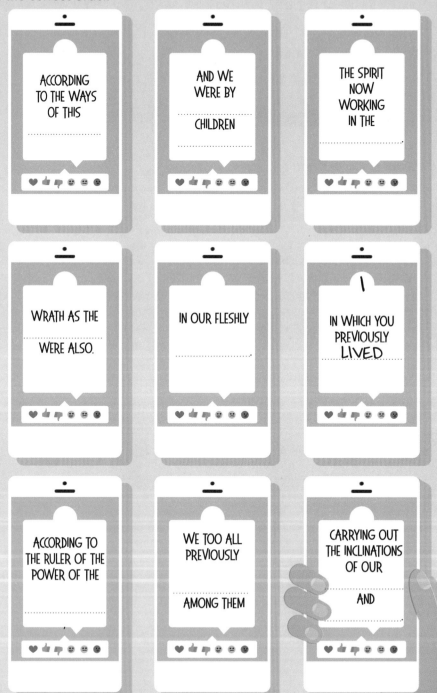

ACCORDING TO THE WAYS OF THIS

AND WE WERE BY
CHILDREN

THE SPIRIT NOW WORKING IN THE

WRATH AS THE
WERE ALSO.

IN OUR FLESHLY

IN WHICH YOU PREVIOUSLY LIVED

ACCORDING TO THE RULER OF THE POWER OF THE

WE TOO ALL PREVIOUSLY
AMONG THEM

CARRYING OUT THE INCLINATIONS OF OUR
AND

STRAIGHT AHEAD, WRONG WAY

The Holy Spirit helps people want to act more and more like Jesus. Satan wants people to act less like Jesus.

Below are examples of things kids sometimes want to do. Draw a line from each one to the proper sign of whether the action leads straight ahead to being more like Jesus or is the wrong way to being more like Jesus.

PRAY FOR A FRIEND

ARGUE OVER THE TV REMOTE

SPEAK WITH KINDNESS

READ OR THINK ABOUT BIBLE VERSES EVERY DAY

DO THE SAME TO SOMEONE WHO HURT YOU

SHARE WHAT YOU HAVE

IGNORE KIDS WHO ARE DIFFERENT THAN YOU

INVITE OTHERS TO CHURCH

DIGGING DEEPER

Find John 14:26 in a Bible. This verse tells two more things the Holy Spirit does. Can you find them?

1) ....

2) ....

Who sent the Holy Spirit? ....

Sometimes different names are used for the Holy Spirit. What name for the Holy Spirit do you find in John 14:26? ....

The names Counselor, Comforter, and Advocate are all names for the Holy Spirit and mean about the same thing. You probably already know the words counselor and comforter, but what about advocate? An advocate is one who is called alongside to help. The Holy Spirit is called to come alongside Christians to help them. Other verses to help you know more about the Holy Spirit are John 14:16-17 and John 16:8.

WALKING IN THE SPIRIT

MY DAILY JOURNAL

A journal is a place to keep track of your thoughts, feelings, questions, answers, and prayers. During the study, these pages will guide you to use your Bible, to think about what you read, and to give you suggestions for prayer.

DAY 1

READ GALATIANS 5:16-17

What do you think is meant by "walking in the Spirit?" ....

....

....

These verses talk about people wanting to do things that are of the world or of the flesh, meaning they want to do what Satan wants. That is not walking in the Spirit! Walking in the Spirit is doing the opposite of what Satan wants. What are some things you know God wants people to do? ....

....

Thank God that the Holy Spirit can help Christians obey God even when they are tempted to disobey. ....

....

DAY 2

READ GALATIANS 5:22-23

These verses list the good results of walking in the Spirit. Write your own list here. Write the first three on the first line, the next three on the second line, and the last three words on the last line.

1) ....

2) ....

3) ....

Thank God that He gives the fruit of the Spirit to those who follow Jesus.

....

....

....

DAY 3

READ EPHESIANS 5:1

What does this verse say to you?

How can you live wisely?

Pray: Thank You, God, for helping me....

DAY 4

READ EPHESIANS 5:18

What should a person be filled with?

Do you think a person filled with the Holy Spirit would act differently than someone who is not? How?

Think about ways the Holy Spirit helps believers. Do you need help from the Holy Spirit? Talk to God about your needs and desires.

DAY 5

READ EPHESIANS 5:20

This verse directs people to give thanks. From the verse, answer the following questions about giving thanks.

When? ....

....

To whom? ....

....

For what? ....

....

How? ....

....

You may have heard people end their prayers by saying "In Jesus' name, Amen." They are remembering to do what this verse encourages. They are praying in the name of Jesus, the One who goes to God for them with their prayers. (Romans 8:34)

When you pray today, remember the what, when, to whom, for what, and how of praying.

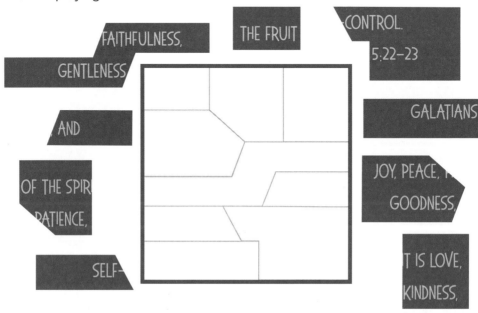

FAITHFULNESS, GENTLENESS THE FRUIT CONTROL. 5:22–23 GALATIANS AND JOY, PEACE, GOODNESS, OF THE SPIRIT PATIENCE, SELF- T IS LOVE, KINDNESS,

What is God teaching you about Himself this week? What have you learned about yourself? Is there anything you need to spend time praying to God about?

Use this journal page to write out your prayers and any thoughts you have about what God is teaching you this week. Thank Him for teaching you through His Word.

Living on Mission

MISSION —
An assigned task

Jesus told His followers to make disciples of other people.
He also promised to be with them to the end of
the age as they worked on
their mission.

KNOW

God has given us
everything we need
to live on mission
with Him.

UNDERSTAND

We have a real
enemy who wants
to discourage us
from fulfilling
our mission.

DISCOVER

Our mission is to
make disciples of
all nations by the
power of the
Holy Spirit.

JESUS GAVE THE GREAT COMMISSION

After Jesus had been raised from the dead, He met with His disciples over the next 40 days. During that time, Jesus told them even more about God's kingdom. Then Jesus' eleven disciples went to a mountain in Galilee.

When the disciples saw Jesus, some of them worshiped Him. But some of the disciples still doubted. Then Jesus went up to them and said, "All authority has been given to Me in heaven and on earth." Jesus is God the Son; He always has authority. But after Jesus died on the cross and rose from the dead, God gave Him all authority in heaven and on earth. Jesus is the King over all creation, and He rules over God's kingdom.

Jesus gave the disciples—and everyone who follows Him—a job to do. He said, "Go into all the world and preach the gospel. Make disciples of people from every nation." A disciple is a follower. Jesus wants His followers to tell people all over the world how to be rescued from sin and death by trusting in Jesus' death and resurrection. Then those people who believe would become disciples of Jesus too.

Jesus also said, "Baptize them in the name of the Father and of the Son and of the Holy Spirit." When believers are baptized, they show the world that they have turned from sin and trusted in Jesus as their Savior. Jesus continued, "Teach them to obey everything I have commanded you." Disciples who love Jesus will want to obey Him. Then Jesus said, "Remember this: I am always with you, until the very end of the age."

Jesus also said, "You will receive power when the Holy Spirit has come on you. You will be My witnesses in Jerusalem, in all Judea and Samaria, and to the ends of the earth."

After Jesus said these things, He went up into heaven. The disciples watched Jesus until a cloud hid Him from their sight. All of the sudden, two men appeared. The men were wearing white clothes. These men asked the disciples, "Men of Galilee, why do you stand looking up into heaven? This Jesus, who has been taken from you into heaven, will come again. He will return in the same way that you have seen Him going into heaven."

—*based on Matthew 28:16-20 and Acts 1:4-14*

GAME DAY

Cross out the stadium seats that contain words that are not found in Ephesians 2:1-10. Color the seats that contain words that are in the verse. Use those words as you try to repeat Ephesians 2:1-10 by memory. Can't do it? Just keep practicing!

TRESPASSES · ~~RUN~~ · SAVED BY GRACE · HAVE ALSO RECEIVED

TREES · #1 · CHRIST JESUS

RULER OF THE POWER · SPORTS · WORKMANSHIP · GOOD WORKS

RICH IN MERCY · GREAT LOVE FOR US · ALIVE WITH CHRIST · JUGS AND JARS · FELLOWSHIP

🔦 DIGGING DEEPER

Read Isaiah 59:17 and then read Ephesians 6:14 and 17. What did you notice about the passages?

Isaiah was describing God, but Paul was describing Christians. God gives Christians the same armor He had! A way to explain righteousness is GHTRI INVGLI. Can you unscramble the words of the definition?

How does a Christian know the right way to live? Ephesians 6:17 gives you a big hint!

MISSING LETTERS

What do you need every day? To find out, write a different letter from the list into each blank box to spell a word. The word will be a familiar food or drink. The blank box may be the beginning letter of the word, a middle letter, or the letter at the end of the word. Each letter in the list will only be used once.

When you finish, read down the white boxes to find the answer to the question at the top of the activity.

T	O	M		T	O
	G		A	P	E
	L	I		E	
L	E	M		N	
	B		E	A	D
	S		D	A	
W	A	F		L	E
	E		G		
	T		A	S	T
		A	T	E	

LETTER BANK:

M O G R O O A D R O F

A SOLDIER'S ARMOR

This soldier is dressed as a Roman soldier of Bible times. Use the list of armor names and write in the correct name on the blank line leading to the piece of armor. (You won't need all the armor names!) Then use your Bible to locate Ephesians 6:14-17. Find the different pieces of armor in the verses. On each line leading to a piece of armor, write the purpose of the armor. Remember that all Christians, kids through adults, have the armor of God!

PIECES OF ARMOR
SHIELD
KNEE PADS
HELMET
BELT
CANTEEN
SWORD
SHOES
CHEST PROTECTOR
BACKPACK

MY DAILY JOURNAL

A journal is a place to keep track of your thoughts, feelings, questions, answers, and prayers. During the study, these pages will guide you to use your Bible, to think about what you read, and to give you suggestions for prayer.

DAY 1

READ MATTHEW 28:18-20

Who spoke these words? ....

The disciples were seeing and hearing Jesus after His resurrection. Jesus was teaching the disciples (and us) something very important.

How do you think these verses apply to you? What did Jesus promise?

....

....

....

Thank God for Jesus' promise to be with believers till the end of the age. ....

....

....

....

DAY 2

READ ACTS 1:8

Who spoke these words? (Verse 6 can give you a hint.) ....

What did Jesus promise the believers? ....

....

What mission did Jesus give the believers? ....

....

How might Jesus want you to obey this verse? ....

....

Talk to Jesus about ways you can obey Him and ask His help in carrying out your mission.

DAY 3

READ EPHESIANS 6:10-12

How strong do you think God is?

Think about God strengthening you. Why, according to verse 11, will God strengthen you?

Some people think the devil is a fictional person, but the Bible clearly shows that the devil is real, deceitful, sly, and evil. But don't be afraid! God is way more powerful than the devil!

Thank God today for His power and might in helping you stand against the devil.

DAY 4

READ EPHESIANS 6:14-15

Think about these three pieces of the Armor of God. How could each of these help you withstand the devil?

TRUTH: ....

....

RIGHTEOUSNESS (RIGHT LIVING): ....

....

READINESS: ....

....

Think about these verses and then talk to God about them. ....

....

....

....

DAY 5

READ EPHESIANS 6:16-18

One important protection for Christians is mentioned that is not often considered a piece of God's armor. What is it? (verse 18) ....

....

How do you think that protection is important for Christians? ....

....

When you pray today, think about reasons for praying. Ask God to help you remember to pray to Him about your everyday life as well as about special times you need help. ....

....

....

....

What is God teaching you about Himself this week? What have you learned about yourself? Is there anything you need to spend time praying to God about?

Use this journal page to write out your prayers and any thoughts you have about what God is teaching you this week. Thank Him for teaching you through His Word.

Parent Guide

DEFINED

Created by God

God made people in His image and for His glory. As the Creator, God determines the purpose of His creation. He has the authority to define what is true about His creation—including people. Your identity is who God says you are.

Key Verse: Ephesians 2:10
Key Passage: God Created People (Genesis 1–2)

BIBLE STORY

Together read the Bible story on page 7 of your child's Activity Book and ask the following review questions.

> **Q1:** What day of creation did God make people?
> **A1:** On the 6th day (Gen. 1:26-27, 31)
> **Q2:** How did God create Adam?
> **A2:** He formed Adam from the dust and breathed life into him. (Gen. 2:7)
> **Q3:** How did God create Eve?
> **A3:** God put Adam into a deep sleep. He took one of his ribs and made a woman. (Gen. 2:21-22)
> **Q4:** How did God make people?
> **A4:** God made people in His image and for His glory. (Gen. 1:27, Col. 1:16)

DEEPER STUDY

Read Ephesians 1 together and discuss the questions.

> **Q1:** When did God plan for people?
> **A1:** Before He created the world (Eph. 1:4)

> **Q2:** What can Jesus provide for a person?
> **A2:** Redemption and forgiveness from sin according to His grace (Eph. 1:7)
> **Q3:** What did God put Jesus above?
> **A3:** Everything (Eph. 1:20-22)
> **Q4:** Who has the authority to determine your identity?
> **A4:** God
> **Q5:** What does it mean to be created in God's image?
> **A5:** When we say God created us in His image, it means we have many similar qualities to God. He gave us these qualities so that we can glorify Him in unique ways.

PRAY AND JOURNAL

Thank God for planning for you before He created the world. Praise Him for creating you uniquely in His image. Ask Him to help you as you live for His glory.

Encourage your child to complete the daily Bible study and journal pages in the activity book this week.

Broken by Sin

This week focuses on our identity broken by sin. God created all people in His image and for His glory, but we have sinned and rebelled against God. Sin separates us from God, but God still loves us. God promised a Rescuer would come from Eve's family. God sent His Son, Jesus, to rescue people from sin and bring them back to God.

Key Verse: Ephesians 2:1
Key Passage: Sin Entered the World (Genesis 3)

BIBLE STORY

Together read the Bible story on page 15 of your child's Activity Book and ask the following review questions.

> **Q1:** What did the serpent first say to Eve?
> **A1:** "Did God really say, 'You can't eat from any tree in the garden?'" *(Gen. 3:1)*
> **Q2:** What did the serpent say would happen if Eve ate the fruit?
> **A2:** She would not die. She would be like God, knowing good and evil. *(Gen. 3:5)*
> **Q3:** What happened after Adam and Eve ate the fruit?
> **A3:** They realized what they had done. They tried to cover themselves and hide from God. *(Gen. 3:7-8)*

DEEPER STUDY

Read Ephesians 2:1-5 together and discuss the following questions.
> **Q1:** What does it mean to sin?
> **A1:** To sin is to think, say, or behave in any way that goes against God and His commands

> **Q2:** Why do you think Adam and Eve sinned?
> **A2:** Adam and Eve did not trust God's plan and they disobeyed God.
> **Q3:** What do these verses tell us about our sin?
> **A3:** Because of our sins, we are separated from God and our identity is broken.
> **Q4:** Read Eph. 2:4-5. What hope do these verses give us about our identity?
> **A4:** God is merciful and loves us. He sent Jesus for us to be forgiven of our sin when we trust in Him.

PRAY AND JOURNAL

Pray together, thanking God for showing you through His Word what is true about all people because of sin. Thank Him for sending Jesus to rescue us from sin when we trust in Him.

Encourage your child to complete the daily Bible study and journal pages in the activity book this week.

Transformed by the Gospel

When we trust in Jesus, we aren't just saying that we agree with the idea of Jesus as God's Son. Through the gospel, God opens our eyes to who Jesus really is. We put our trust in Him, believing that His death on the cross provides forgiveness for our sins and that because He was raised from the dead, He is King over everything. When we trust in Jesus, He changes our hearts. He removes our identity of sin and gives us a new identity—child of God!

Key Verse: Ephesians 2:8-9
Key Passage: Saul's Conversion (Acts 8–9)

BIBLE STORY

Together read the Bible story on page 23 of your child's Activity Book and ask the following review questions.

> **Q1:** What did Saul intend to do in Damascus?
> **A1:** Arrest Christians *(Acts 9:2)*
> **Q2:** What happened to Saul on the way to Damascus?
> **A2:** A light blinded him, and Jesus spoke to him. *(Acts 9:3-6)*
> **Q3:** God told Ananias He had a plan for Saul. What was God's plan?
> **A3:** To tell the Gentiles about Jesus *(Acts 9:15)*
> **Q4:** What did Saul begin to do after he could see again?
> **A4:** To speak in the synagogues about Jesus *(Acts 9:20)*

DEEPER STUDY

Read Ephesians 2:1-10 together and discuss the following questions.

> **Q1:** This passage teaches us about sin. What does it mean that we sinned against God?

> **A1:** God cannot be around sin. Sin separates us from God and deserves God's punishment of death. *(Eph. 2:1-3; Romans 6:23)*
> **Q2:** What did God provide for us?
> **A2:** God provided His Son Jesus to rescue us from the punishment we deserve. *(Eph. 2:4-5)*
> **Q3:** What is God's salvation?
> **A3:** God's salvation is a gift that every person needs and can receive. *(Eph 2:8-9)*
> **Q4:** What happens when a person trusts in Jesus for salvation?
> **A4:** When someone trusts in Jesus as Savior, her whole identity is transformed!

PRAY AND JOURNAL

Pray with your child, thanking God for sending Jesus. Praise Him for rescuing people who are dead in their sin and making them alive.

Encourage your child to complete the daily pages in the activity book this week. Be available to answer any questions about the gospel or trusting in Jesus for salvation.

Who We Are in Christ

God defines the true identity of all followers of Jesus. When we trust in Jesus for salvation, our identity is changed and transformed by the gospel. Like fruit grows when it is connected to the vine, Christians grow to look more like Jesus when we are connected to Him. Jesus rescues us from sin and frees us to live a life that honors God. By doing what is good and right, people who trust Jesus can show that they really believe in Him.

Key Verse: Ephesians 2:4-5
Key Passage: The Vine and the Branches (John 15:1-8)

BIBLE STORY

Together read the Bible story on page 31 of your child's Activity Book and ask the following review questions.

> **Q1:** Who is the true vine and gardener in this story?
> **A1:** Jesus is the true vine and God the Father is the gardener *(John 15:1)*
> **Q2:** Who does Jesus say are the branches?
> **A2:** The branches are people who trust in Jesus. *(John 15:5)*
> **Q3:** How did the branches produce fruit in Jesus' parable?
> **A3:** The branches stayed connected to Jesus to produce fruit. *(John 15:4-5)*

Comment that Jesus told this parable or story about the vine and branches to help His disciples understand that they are now transformed, or changed because they trust in Jesus. Jesus referred to their hearts changing—their identity.

DEEPER STUDY

Read Ephesians 2:1-5 together and discuss the following questions.

> **Q1:** What does God teach you through these verses?
> **A1:** All people sin against God and are separated from Him, but God provided Jesus so we can be saved through grace
> **Q2:** What does the word adopted mean?
> **A2:** Adoption is when God welcomes us into His family as His children.
> **Q3:** How can Christians grow to look more like Jesus?
> **A3:** By obeying God's Word, saying no to sin with the help of the Holy Spirit, and loving others like Jesus loves Christians can show others we really believe in Jesus.

PRAY AND JOURNAL

Pray together, asking God for His help to abide in Him, say no to sin, and love others like Jesus loves.

Encourage your child to complete the daily pages in the activity book this week. Be available to answer any questions throughout the week.

What We Have in Christ

Jesus came to seek and save the lost. Explain that people sometimes use the word lost to describe people whose identity is broken by sin and without God, those who have not trusted Jesus as their Savior. Jesus taught people that He came to save people from their sins. Just like people are happy when something lost is found, all of heaven is happy when a person turns from sin to trusting in Jesus.

Key Verse: Ephesians 2:5-6
Key Passage: Jesus Taught Three Parables

BIBLE STORY

Together read the Bible story on page 39 of your child's Activity Book and ask the following review questions.

> **Q1:** Jesus spent time teaching people whom the religious leaders did not like. Who were they?
> **A1:** Sinners and tax collectors *(Luke 15:2)*
> **Q2:** What did that man do when he found his lost sheep?
> **A2:** He invited his friends and neighbors to celebrate with him. *(Luke 15:6)*
> **Q3:** What did the woman do when she lost one of her coins?
> **A3:** She lit a lamp and searched the house carefully until she found it. *(Luke 15:8)*
> **Q4:** How did the father greet the younger son in the third parable when he returned home?
> **A4:** He greeted his son warmly, joyfully, lovingly, and with compassion. *(Luke 15:20)*

DEEPER STUDY

Read Ephesians 1:3-8 and 13 and discuss the following questions.

> **Q1:** Read verses 3-8 and complete the following statements: I am _____; I am _____; I am _____; I am _____; I am _____; I am _____. Discuss the meaning of each of these identities with your child.
> **A1:** I am blessed, I am chosen, I am adopted, I am redeemed, I am forgiven, I am sealed.
> **Q2:** Which one of these statements is easiest or more difficult to identify with and believe? Explain.
> **A2:** Answers will vary.

PRAY AND JOURNAL

Pray with your child, thanking God for all of the spiritual blessings He gives us in Jesus when we trust in Him. Ask Him to help your family remember your identity this week— who God says you are.

Encourage your child to complete the daily Bible study and journal pages this week. Be available to answer any questions throughout the week.

Living Out Our Identity

Some people think the Bible is mostly just rules about what to do and what not to do. While there certainly are instructions about how to live, the Bible is not just a list of rules God wants us to follow. The gospel transforms us from the inside out. Our minds and hearts change to understand God better and love Him more, and then our behavior changes because of our new thoughts and new desires.

Key Verse: Ephesians 2:2-3
Key Passage: Peter Denied Jesus and Was Forgiven (Luke 22:31-34; 54-62; John 21:1-19; Acts 2)

BIBLE STORY

Together read the Bible story on page 47 of your child's Activity Book and ask the following review questions.

> **Q1:** What did Peter do three times before the rooster crowed?
> **A1:** Peter denied Jesus. *(Luke 22:54-60)*
> **Q2:** When Peter realized that he had denied Jesus, what did he do?
> **A2:** Peter went outside and wept bitterly. *(Luke 22:62)*
> **Q3:** What question did Jesus ask Peter three times?
> **A3:** "Peter, do you love me?" *(John 21:15, 16, 17)*
> **Q4:** How did Peter answer Jesus' questions?
> **A4:** "Yes, Lord. You know I love You." *(John 21:15, 16, 17)*
> **Q5:** What did Peter do when people heard the disciples speaking in many languages?
> **A5:** He stood up and preached to the people, telling them that Jesus was the Messiah. *(Acts 2:14)*

DEEPER STUDY

Read Ephesians 4:22-24 together and discuss the following questions.

> **Q1:** What did Paul mean when He talked about the "old self"?
> **A1:** Paul meant that Christians have a new identity in Jesus.
> **Q2:** What does it mean to put on the "new self"?
> **A2:** Putting on the "new self" means choosing actions that look more like Jesus. Our minds and hearts change to understand God better and love Him more, and then our behavior changes because of our new thoughts and new desires.
> **Q3:** What does verse 24 teach us about this "new self"?
> **A3:** The "new self" was created according to God's likeness in righteousness and purity of truth.

PRAY AND JOURNAL

Pray together, thanking God for teaching your child what it looks like to live out the Christian life. Praise God for always forgiving us of our sin and sending the Holy Spirit to help guide us as we live for God's glory.

When we trust in Jesus, the Holy Spirit begins to change us. Paul told the believers in the Galatian church how to recognize that God is working in someone's life. People who are saved by Jesus become more like Him, and the Holy Spirit gives them power to say no to sin and to live in a way that pleases God.

Key Verse: Ephesians 2:2-3
Key Passage: The Fruit of the Spirit (Galatians 5)

BIBLE STORY

Read the Bible story for Session 7 on page 55 of your child's Activity Book and ask the following review questions.

> **Q1:** Who did Paul write this letter to?
> **A1:** The church at Galatia *(Gal. 1:2)*
> **Q2:** When the Holy Spirit is in control, what actions to people choose?
> **A2:** Love, joy, peace, patience, kindness, goodness, faithfulness, gentleness, and self-control. *(Gal. 5:22-23)*
> **Q3:** What does the fruit of the Spirit mean?
> **A3:** These actions are proof that the Spirit is in someone. The more we know Jesus, the more we choose these actions.

DEEPER STUDY

Mention that the Bible helps us know at least three things about the Holy Spirit: The Holy Spirit comforts us, shows us our sin, and guides us as we live for God's glory. Read the following verses and discuss.

> **Q1:** Read John 16:13 together. Who is the "Spirit of truth"? What did Jesus say He would do when He came?
> **A1:** The "Spirit of truth" is the Holy Spirit. Jesus told His followers that the Holy Spirit would guide them.
> **Q2:** Read John 16:8 together. What else does the Holy Spirit do?
> **A2:** The Holy Spirit shows us our sin.
> **Q3:** Read Ephesians 5:15 together. What does this verse instruct believers to do?
> **A3:** This verse tells believers to live wisely. Believers can live wisely by praying to God, reading and obeying the Bible, trusting in God's promises, and growing to look more like Jesus.

PRAY AND JOURNAL

Pray together, thanking God for His Word to teach your family more about the Holy Spirit. Ask the Holy Spirit to comfort you, show you sin in your life, and guide your family as you live for God's glory.

Encourage your child to complete the daily pages this week.

Living on Mission

Jesus gave the disciples the Great Commission, but it wasn't just for them. It is a command for all of us. Every person who believes in Jesus has a responsibility to share the gospel—the good news about Jesus. Our mission is to make disciples of all nations by the power of the Holy Spirit.

Key Verse: Ephesians 2:10
Key Passage: Jesus Gave the Great Commission (Matthew 28:16-20; Acts 1:4-14)

BIBLE STORY

Read the Bible story for Session 8 on page 63 of your child's Activity Book and ask the following review questions.

> **Q1:** What had been given to Jesus in heaven and on earth?
> **A1:** All authority *(Matt. 28:18)*
> **Q2:** What was the job Jesus had for His disciples?
> **A2:** Go make disciples of all nations, baptizing them in the name of the Father, the Son, and the Holy Spirit, teaching them to observe everything He has commanded them. *(Matt. 28:19)*
> **Q3:** What was the last thing Jesus told them?
> **A3:** He would be with them. *(Matt. 28:20)*
> **Q4:** What is our mission?
> **A4:** Our mission as believers is to make disciples of all nations by the power of the Holy Spirit.

DEEPER STUDY

Read Ephesians 6:10-20 together. Remind your child that the armor of God is not a physical armor that we carry around or wear. The armor Paul talks about was his way of communicating the protection God gives believers to live on mission. Discuss the following questions.

> **Q1:** How does learning about the armor of God encourage us?
> **A1:** Learning about the armor of God reminds us that God has given us everything we need to live on mission for Him.
> **Q2:** Who is our battle against?
> **A2:** Our battle is against Satan and the powers of evil.
> **Q3:** Besides putting on the armor of God, what did Paul tell the church to do?
> **A3:** He told the church to pray at all times in the Spirit.

PRAY AND JOURNAL

Lead your child in prayer, thanking God for giving us what we need to live on mission and stand strong against evil. Pray that God would guide your family to fight the good fight and expand His kingdom.

Encourage your child to complete the daily pages in the activity book this week. Look back with your child and discuss what God has taught him through this study.

CERTIFICATE OF COMPLETION

THIS CERTIFICATE IS AWARDED TO

ON

DATE

FOR COMPLETING

DEFINED

WHO GOD SAYS YOU ARE

PARENT OR LEADER'S SIGNATURE